Abou~~t~~ ~~this book~~

MW00398419

The essence of this book is the focus on the love of God that surrounds us. With your heart and mind set on the love that is around you, the lies that confound you are dispelled.

Inspired by the Holy Spirit, these writings are all about God's Love and are Mark's gift back to the One who first loved us. Within this book you'll find writings similar to the Psalms.

It contains personal verses written to God, for and about God, spanning twenty years of Mark's spiritual walk through life with Him.

There are also brief insights describing what Godly loving and living is, that you may find helpful with the daily trials of life that you may be facing, as well as with your spiritual journey.

We are "Surrounded by His Love" not by enemies. We are not captives - we have been freed.

Scripture footnotes have been added to each writing, opening up a much broader understanding of their contents. The rhythm, rhyme and brevity of these writings will allow you to absorb the heart and healing of the messages.

The layout of the book is truly a love concordance as well as an interactive scripture guide for the reader to meditate on and to write their own affirmations and thoughts of love.

Because Mark carries the song of the Lord in his heart, most of the writings have melodies within them. If you listen carefully in your spirit, you will also hear the love of God resonating within your heart as you read them. You may find yourself singing them.

This book is prefaced with "Seeds of Love" which are small pieces from within this book, to plant within your heart.

Surrounded by His Love

His Desire for Your heart

Mark C Ettinger

Copyright 2012

All Rights Reserved

282 West Main Street
Hummelstown, PA 17036
717-599-1680
Markssong@verizon.net
Books are available via e-mail or www.Hegai.org

All scripture verses used as a reference or in poetic form
have been extracted from the King James Version and converted
to present day English or paraphrased by the author.

All lyrical writings may be used by permission only.

Open spaces have been provided throughout this book for you to interact and write your inspired messages, your affirmations and thoughts of love. Reading with an open heart and waiting patiently, you will hear from God. He also wants to hear your heart, so please write your thoughts and share them with others - letting the fruit of your love bloom.

I believe that patience, one of the fruits of the spirit in (*Galatians 5:22*) is one of the most rewarding . Patience itself, brings you closer to joy, peace, kindness, goodness, gentleness, faithfulness, endurance and self-control. Oh yes, and love, which in itself contains all of the fruits.

In (*1 Corinthians 13:4*) we are told: "Love is patient." I've learned that as we practice patience, our love for one another will bloom.

An Invitation

Sacrificing your life for the life of another is the greatest act of love. Forgiveness is equally as great. Combine these two into one event and you'll find Jesus. He sacrificed Himself and became our source of forgiveness, opening Heaven's door to those who don't know God. "Whoever is forgiven much, will love much." (*Luke 7:47*) I have been forgiven much and this book is the fruit of God's love and forgiveness. If you have never realized His forgiveness, take a moment and breathe in His love. Tell Him that you receive Him as the source of the air you breathe - as the source of eternal life. Ask to be forgiven much - God is willing and faithful to forgive. "Everyone who calls on the name of the Lord, will be saved (*Romans 10:13*) paraphrased.

"If we say we have no sin, we deceive ourselves and the truth is not in us. If we confess our sins to Him, He is faithful and just to forgive us our sins and to cleanse us from all unrighteousness. (*1 John 1:8-9*) paraphrased You are loved with an everlasting love. For God so loved the world, that He sent a final sacrifice from Himself, in the form of a son - in His image. Not one that could die, but live forever. A sacrifice not made or chosen or given by man but by God Himself, to redeem those who had departed from what He had begun, and those who did not know God. Whoever believes and chooses to follow Him, will be saved from death and have eternal life with Him.

(*John 3:16* - *Hebrews 9:15, 24*) paraphrased. Continue reading this book with His love and forgiveness caressing your heart and watch your love grow.

Seeds of Love

(Plant them within your heart)

*Focus on love and you'll be
surrounded by love

* It's all about His love

*The love song of redemption
is the power of His affection

*He loves His plan and He plans His love

*There is nothing that can separate me
from Your endless love

*I will have peace - because You love me

*Let His love overwhelm you

*When I'm facing adversity
You surround me

*His love flows on and on
when we think His love is gone

*Send your rain - shower us with love
let your love pour down upon us Lord

*You are with me when I cry
speaking truth when evil lies

*You saw me - You heard me
You love me - You chose me

*His love never ends

*You love me as I am

*Your love covers me, like a soft morning dew
and it's raining - raining from You

*You have become my first love
all because You first loved me

*I want to live the words that I sing
then His word will be living

*The Spirit is love

*When my love is unsure
You love me even more
my broken heart restored
because I am adored

*I must come to You for love
for Your love has come to me

*When I go astray - You love me

*Help me think love - Help me be love
help me speak love - Help me feel love
only love - God you are love

*I am so amazed - at the love He has for me

*Dear Jesus, I love you

*You have been my loving kindness
took away all of my blindness

*Love is the answer

*I am my beloved's - my beloved is mine
He has been my lover since before I knew time

*Keep me in your will - help me to be still
In your love

*I would stay with You forever
by the stillness of Your water

*Your love that always covers me
that is such a mystery

*I want to smell your love
like a Holy perfume

*Drinking in the love that You give
filling up my spirit within

*You in me - is my reward

*His Holy Spirit among us is poetry
His love for you is poetry
God - You are poetry

*Feel His touch - He's holding you
you're the one He loves

*For He so loved the world
how could I not love the world

*The next time you need to feel God's love

love a person near you

*Love is freedom
freedom to love - free to be loved

*I love the Jesus in you -
I love the life He gives through you

*The essence of love -

As God has forgiven you - forgive others

Love is His Love

Contents

Highlighted titles are introductions.

Chapter One

His love

Introduction

What God says is love, and what He did for us with His love, surpasses anything that we could ever express with the love we have within us. Only laying down your life for another can begin to compare to His love. He wants to be the greatest lover and source of love that we know. To even try to out- love God, would be in vain. (*1 John 4:10*)

When we concede to that, we relinquish our pride or claim to being our own source of great love and we will attribute it to the creator of love itself. Love then becomes less selfish, less lustful, less driven, less resentful, more prolific and more imitable. We can be imitators. (*Ephesians 5:1*)

My prayer and greatest desire is that you absorb the fullness of what God has been sharing with me for twenty years, each time you read this book. I pray that you are as blessed by reading it as I was by writing it and that you feel drawn to reference it with your Bible. The writing of this book led me deeper into the love in God's word and loving Him and His word even more.

God's love is present in the shallow waters, though you can go deeper and seek the depth of His love. Let Him find you there, searching the depths of the sea of His love, where He will show you hidden treasures.

Love is His love

Love is the sunrise that met me this morning [1]
Love is the rainfall - I love when it's pouring

I don't know where it comes from - but from above
I don't know what I'd become - without His love

Love is the length of this life that I'm living [2]
Love is God's mercy and grace and forgiving

All of the wrong that I've done - vanished by love [3]
Healing the wounds left undone
God healed this one

Life is love's picture - God is the frame
Love is a savior - Jesus His name

Love is the ocean - kissing the shore [4]
Love is the one thing - we all adore
We all want more

I don't know where it comes from - but from above
I don't know what I'd become - without His love
Love is His love

1. Lamentations 3:21-23
2. Job 14:16, Jeremiah 32:19, Psalm 56:8, 90:12, 139:1-4
3. Psalm 103:12   4. Job 38:11

3

I'm Overwhelmed

I'm overwhelmed - by the depth of your love
and how much you give to me
I'm overwhelmed - by the price that you paid
and gave it to me for free [1]

I'm so in awe of you - at times don't know what to do
I'm overwhelmed - and I'm starting to see
that you're overwhelmed with me

I'm overwhelmed - that your mercy endures
and your goodness is there for me

I'm overwhelmed - when my faithfulness fails
that your faith is still with me

I'm overwhelmed - You're overwhelmed with me
So overwhelmed, that you're a part of me
I'm overwhelmed - by the depth of your love
and how much you give to me

1. 1Cor.2:12, Romans 8:32

Note: I was so overwhelmed by all the references for this verse.
Please know that God *has given* so much to us, that I can't fit it all
at the bottom of this page. You would do well to do a word search in the
scriptures on the word "give" and be in awe, for all we have
been given - *freely*.

4

All about Your Love

You are the answer - to all of my fears [1]
You're my romancer - through all of the years
You have prepared a new table for me
All in the presence of my enemies [2]

And it's all - all about - Your love for me [3]

My strength and my heart - they may fail
Your strength and your heart - will prevail [4]
I look to the heavens - You are there
I'm not just your servant - I'm an heir [5]

You are a picture - of how things will be
Already knowing - what you've done for me [6]
Day after day - You help me to see
You've made me an heir of Your victory [7]

And it's all - all about - Your love for me
It's all - all about - Your love for me

1. Psalm 27:1, 34:4
2. Psalm 23:5
3. Deut. 4:37, John 3:16, Revelation 21:3-4
4. Psalm 73:25-26
5. Galatians 4, Romans 8:17
6. Revelation 1:8
7. 1 Cor. 15:55, 1 John 5:4

By His great love

(for those who don't yet know God)

He is the Lord of all - He blesses all
Who call on His name to be saved [1]
With Him we're all the same - and by His name
We'll never be put into shame

Now the Word is in you - It's in your mouth
It hides in your heart- It's so near
The Word is Jesus - The Son of God
And you'll be a son if you hear [2]
So confess with your mouth - Believe in your heart
That Jesus is Lord and was raised
Then the Lord will believe you
And He will receive you
And by His great love - You'll be saved
Yes by His great love - You'll be saved

Now the Message is living - It walks with you
How beautiful is the Good News
So they will believe you
And they will receive you
And Jesus is whom they will choose

1. Romans 10:8-13, John 17:21
2. John 1:12, Romans 8:14

6

Love song of Redemption

(for those who don't yet know God)

Have you heard the revelation - all about the Resurrection
And what it is that Jesus did for you [1]
There's a story that foretold Him [2]
There's a grave that could not hold Him [3]
So you'd realize that He did rise for you

It's a love song of redemption
Of the power of His affection
Your salvation rests at Heaven's open door
The world brought you affliction
The Lord brought crucifixion
So you don't have to suffer anymore [4]

Now just call the Name of Jesus [5]
He's the one that came to save us
All of Heaven is rejoicing over you [6]
You won't miss the life you're living
You will love the life He's giving
And you'll realize- that He did rise for you
And you'll see the place that He prepared for you [7]
It's a love song of redemption over you

1. John 11:25, 1 Corinthians 15:1-28
2. Isaiah 53:1-12, Zechariah 12:10
3. Matthew 28:1-10
4. 2 Corinthians 1:4, Romans 5:8
5. Romans 10:12, Acts 2:21
6. Luke 15:4-10
7. Matthew 25:34

7

Divine Intervention

The way that you define and value love, give and receive love, is determined by the impact that God's love has had upon your life. It will determine also, the impact that your love has upon other's lives. Is your love making an impression on people? God's love makes loving easy.

I was once in a place of feeling loveless and unloved and on the verge of suicide, when God Himself, stepped between me and death and said: "Enough". That was Divine intervention.

Feeling sorry for myself and for what happened to me could not change my life.

Worldly sorrow is not equal to Godly sorrow. The world will watch your demise. God will change you - give you life. The Godly will forgive through love. (*2 Corinthians 7:9,10*)

I love the events of God's Divine intervention - Kairos moments - unsolicited acts of love that happen at the precise moment they need to, for His plan to be fulfilled.

He loves His plan and He plans His love.

The story of Balaam and Balak is one of my favorite examples of God's intervention and how it totally frustrates the enemy as it happens. Especially when the one intending to curse is blessed.

Balaam was blessed by speaking a blessing he didn't want to speak. God told him that he will speak only what He told him to speak.

Neither riches or the promise of posterity could turn him, and his eyes were opened to God's unchangeable love for His people.

You can read about it and see how he changes the plans of the enemy : (*Numbers 22:10-12 , 24*)
Changes the results the enemy gets:
(*Numbers 23:11-12, 24:1*)
How he determines the future:
(*Numbers 23:8, 19 -23, 24:3-17*)

Speaking blessings changes people for the good. It's a Godly order. *Numbers 23:8, 20*
Divine Intervention - when God's people are blessed, even by those that intended to curse.
Can you think of a time when you were blessed and didn't really know why? Remember Balak.
The power of God's love and the benefits of Godly love are unchallengeable and unchangeable.

The Family of God

I've been born into the family of the Father of Creation
Not just any family but a Holy congregation
The family of God [1]

All creation's singing of the love that He is bringing
The joy that is heard ringing [2]
In the family of God

I am so excited because I am invited [3]
To a place I'll stay forever
With the Father and my Savior

I'll be singing with the Angels
Walking through the Temples
Living in the Glory of the Holiest of Holies

Hearing from my Father
All of creation's stories

Born into the family
Loving me eternally

The family of God

1. Ephesians 2:19
2. Psalm 149:1
3. Revelation 19:9

Nothing like your love

There is nothing that can separate me
From your endless love [1]
Not a thing that lies below me
And nothing from above

Nothing can come before me
That you can't put away
All that you've prepared for me [2]
Is waiting for the day

Nothing can come between the things
That you have planned to do [3]
Nothing I may get caught in
That you can't pull me through [4]

There's nothing that your love can't do
There's nothing like your love
Nothing like your love for me
Nothing like your love

1. Romans 8:38,39
2. 1 Cor. 2:9, Hebrews 11:16,
   Revelation 21:2
3. Isaiah 14: 2
4. Psalm 40:2

11

You said I love you

You sent the rain from a cloudless sky
You brought a tear to a tearless eye
You did this all and you make me sigh

I love You

You said - Light be and the dark was gone [1]
You said - Now see and the blind walked on [2]
You sent your son and my sin was gone [3]

I love You

You said I love you
So it's You whom I love
You said I love you
And I can't get enough

Soon the light will come from Your love [4]
I love You

1. Genesis 1:3
2. Mark 10:51,52
3. John 1:29
4. Isaiah 60;19,20.
Revelation 21:23,24

12

Surrender you're Surrounded

I created you naked - you are naked before Me [1]

I see what I've created -

Not what you have covered

yourself with [2]

You were created beautiful - in My sight - in My Image

You are covered by My love [3]

Arise today - beautiful

Knowing you are clothed with Me - surrounded by Me

Surrender - you're surrounded by My love

1. Genesis 2:25

2. Genesis 3:25

3. Psalm 27:5, Isaiah 4:6

Your Treasure

You have so much love for me
More than I can measure

And the way you feel for me
Just like I'm your treasure

Though I turn away from my first love
You come after me with more love [1]

You bring me back to the love I lost
There's no more complete love
At no greater cost

And it cost me nothing
You paid it all [2]

More than I can measure
Just like I'm your treasure

When I know I'm worth this much
I will know your loving touch

A touch that gives the greatest pleasure
When I know that I'm your greatest treasure

1. Revelation 2:4
2. John 10:18

14

The Rain's Symphony

When I feel the rain upon my face

I feel Your mercy and Your grace

As the rain falls all around me

The countless sounds surround me

The sound of the rain's symphony

Lord, it's Your majesty

The leaves of the trees become instruments

As the raindrops play their song

A melody from Heaven, rains on and on and on

The softest song ever heard - Rain falling through the trees

Unlike a song you only hear - God lets this song be seen

The drops of rain that sound surreal

A song that Heaven lets me feel

As the rain falls all around me

The sound of the rain's symphony

Lord, Your melody rains upon me

The most beautiful love song

Isaiah 55:10,11

Truly Love

What is love - Where is love - Who is love

When is love - Really Love

This is love - That is love - Here is love - There is love

God is love - Really love

He is love - Truly love - God is love

Give His love - Sing His love - Live His love

Bring His love - Truly love

This is love

He is love

Holy Love

Really love

God is love - Truly love

1 John 4:8

Love is a powerful word

The language of love is universal
One language of unspoken words
Understood only as love.. Do you know it?

Yes, love is a powerful word. Words make a visitation. Love, if absorbed, makes a habitation. There is a presence surrounding the word love. Love itself is a connector between human beings and God. God is literally the overseer of the word love. He is the integer of what love is - the multiplication symbol itself. Believing this will simplify your love life with Him. Love is more than just a word.

Actions of love, prove themselves more evidently than simply speaking love. Words of love too often only signify an intent. Jesus did what he said he would do. He literally initiated the term: "I love you to death." Love is visible, yet invisible.

God Himself is invisible, yet the love that He represents is the most visible and the most altruistic. His love is blameless, self-less, unconditional, holds no record of wrongs, and offers total forgiveness and reconciliation to Himself. Forgiveness was His love child - a child that resembled Him - the Father. Love resembles the Father and is understood only as love. Do you know it?

Agape - Unconditional Love

Agape - Unconditional love [1]
Agape - Falls on us from His love
To give you - The love we all dream of

Love will come - Love will go away
When you find love in a physical way
Ask the Lord to share His way
And you'll find love in a Spiritual way [2]

He cares for me - He cares for you
Agape love will pull you through
You will see your heart feels new [3]
When unconditional love finds you

Unconditional love
The love we all dream of

1. Deuteronomy 6:5, Romans 5:8 2. 1 John 2:15-17, John 15:13,

Romans 5:5, 13:10, 2 Cor. 6:6, Galatians 5:13

3. 1 Peter 5:6-7

Because You love me

I will be blessed - because You love me
I will have joy - because You love me
I will have peace - because You love me
You love me

I will love You - because You love me
I will love You -You are the Holy one
I will love You - Your love has made us one [1]
I love You

I will love You
I will be blessed
I will have joy
I will have peace
Full of Your grace
Light on my face
My soul at rest
I can confess - Lord I am blessed
Because You love me

1. John 17:13-23

The depth of your love

You bring light in the morning

And with every dawning

You show me the depth of your love

When your mercy is falling

Your Spirit is calling

Come be here with me in my love

Psalm 17:15

Dance with Me My Beloved

I describe the word intimacy, as a feeling of love and being so drawn and connected to someone, that they are your only focus and you never want to take your eyes off of them, or ever let go of them - only seeing and hearing the one who is with you..

Our Father is calling to us to dance with Him.. Don't wait until that Glorious day when you enter the Wedding Supper. Let Him set you free - do it right now. Call out to the Lover of your soul , in your next time of intimacy " Dance with me my Beloved."
He will dance with you, even if you think you can't dance. He will show you that there are no wrong steps, when you let Him lead. When only the eyes of your Father- your Creator - your Beloved, are watching you - cherishing you- healing you- setting you free.
All you have to say is: 'Dance with me."

Dance with Me - Dance with Me
Dance with Me - My Beloved
Dance with Me - I'll set you free
Dance with Me - My Beloved

Psalm 30:11, 87:7, 149:3
Isaiah 55:10,11

21

God 's Love

God's love is the ocean - God's love is the sky
God's love is its color - Yet I don't know why

God's love is more than the Earth can contain
God's love is the universe that I can't explain

God's love is in every verse of His word [1]
God's love is the song of a beautiful bird

God's love is more than I can comprehend
Were that to be - I might look for the end [2]

God's love is endless - so that I can't see
All He has waiting at the end for me [3]

As deep as the ocean, as blue as the sky
As vast as the universe He has in His eye
This is God's word - This is God's love [4]

1. Jeremiah 1:12
2. Deuteronomy 4:32
3.Matthew 25:34, 1 Corinthians 2:9
4. Psalm 119

Head above the water

How can I feel so far away - You're so close to me
I have nothing to fear - because you are near [1]
When I'm facing adversity
You surround me [2]
Like the endless blue surrounds the clouded sky
A pavilion hovering over me [3]
Under your watchful eye
I'm a son, you are my Father
You keep my head above the water

1. Proverb 17:17
2. Job 1:10, Isaiah 58:8
3. Psalm 27:5

His Love flows on

His love is a river that flows on and on [1]
His love will deliver when we can't go on
His love fills the emptiness we let go dry
His love is the faithfulness we fail to try [2]

His love flows on and on
When we think His love is gone
His love flows on and on
That's why He sent us His Son
His love flows on and on and on and on

His love endures forever
His love goes on forever
So we're forever - together

He never remembers the sins that we've done
He only remembers what Jesus has done
He said they're as far as the east from the west [3]
He said this so all of His children can rest

His love endures forever

1. Psalm 36:8, 46:4
2. 2 Timothy 2:13
3. Psalm 103:12

I know the plans I have for you

For I know the plans I have for you
Plans to prosper and not harm you
You'll have a hope and a future too [1]

I know the plans I have for you
Yes I know the plans I have for you

I'll guide you down the perfect way
Just so I can hear you say
Lord your love is so great and true
I know my plan is to love you too

I know the plans - the plans I made for you
The plans I made to abide in you [2]
The plans to see you be made whole
My love for you is in control
My love for you restores your soul
I know the plans I have for you

1. Jeremiah 29:11

2. John 14:16, 15: 4,7

25

I know you

You've been on the outside, my dark but lovely one [1]
Feeling like a banished flower - wilted by the sun
You've forgotten it's My plan - to marry you one day
Come a little closer to Me - hear the words I say

Speak to me my love - my Bride
I'm your King so come inside [2]
Know you never have to hide from me
Come and sing a sweet love song
Come inside where you belong
Come abide where you'll know more of Me
I'm the One your heart seeks for
I'm the Love you're longing for
I'm the One who knows you more [3]
Than anyone you know
Don't you know that it's my plan
to marry you one day [4]
Don't you know - since time began
I'd carry you away
I've prepared a place for you
I'll do everything for you
There's no need to hide your face
Welcome to my Holy place

1. Song 1:5
2. Song 1:4
3. Jeremiah 1:5
4. Revelation 21:2

Let Your Love Pour Down

Let your love pour down upon us Lord
Let your love pour down upon us Lord
We are dry - shower us with love

Send your rain - shower us with love [1]
We are dry - and we need your love
You fill us up - fill our empty cup [2]
We are dry and we need your love
Let your love pour down upon us Lord

Holy Spirit fill us with your word
Holy Spirit fill us with your word [3]
Hear our cry - help us speak your word
Send your rain - shower us with love
Let your love pour down upon us Lord

1. Hosea 6:3
2. 2 Kings 4:3-7, Psalm 23:5
3. Acts 1:5, 2:4, 33

Speaking a Blessing

How great a love it is, to be born and be the recipient of life sustaining breath, without any of our doing - without our deserving it or earning it. We were born into love.

Meditate on this for a moment; Realize the magnitude of what God is saying to us when he said :

"Love one another, as I have loved you".

(*John 13:34 - 1 John 3:23*) Jesus - His first breath was for us, as was His last breath, for us.

You may not have ever thought of this, but every word that you speak, has a breath powering it. I do regret and had to repent and ask forgiveness for some of the words I've spoken, and I know that it's still within me to say hurtful things, if I was provoked and lost control. I always pray that God would give me the self-control to not feel the need to speak anything hurtful but only that which is loving. We are all capable of speaking blessings or hurtful things. God breathed "life" into us and the last thing we will do on this earth, is breathe out the life within us.

I believe that it was God's intention for us to use our life giving breath, to speak out life and love. Meditate on how you could accomplish that in your daily life, by letting hurtful things go. Who could you speak a blessing over, today? By doing so, you open yourself up to be blessed in return.

"A blessing spoken"

I love the way that His light shines upon you
I love the reflection of the Lord from you
His light warms your fragrance
that He loves to smell
You are the story that He loves to tell
The love you're displaying
The role you're portraying
Your life is a song the Lord is now playing
The love of His light that shines upon you

Feel the blessing - Speak a blessing

Love conquers all

Your loves conquers all
So how can I fall [1]
Against any wall [2]
Your love conquers fear [3]
When darkness draws near
Your love is the light [4]
Your love conquers all

1. Isaiah 54:17, Revelation 1:18
2. Joshua 6:5
3. 2 Timothy 1:17
4. Psalm 139;11,12

30

Peace - Mercy - Love

You are the God of creation and life
The God of peace, mercy and love
You love your creation and its destination
You knew in the beginning and in the end
The direction the days would follow [1]

I am your child - your creation - your life
I am not anything that the world or my
Vain imaginations say that I am [2]
You abide in me and I should abide in you

You live through my heart and my heartbeat is from you
I am the product of peace - mercy and love
I am an heir of your creation and its destination
You've brought me into your banqueting table
And your banner over me is love [3]

1. Revelation 1:8

2. Genesis 8:2, 1 Chronicles 28:9, Psalm 60:11, 2 Cor. 10:5, Romans 1:21

3. Song of Solomon 2:4

31

Your love story

I awoke again - into Your glory

One more page in your love story

As this day unfolds before me

I will pray you will assure me

That you love me

I'm the love in your love story

Genesis 1, John 3, Revelation 3:5

You are with me

When I see a flower grow - Then I can be still and know

You are with me

When I see the light of day - I can look to You and say

You are with me

When I can't see You at all - You still catch me when I fall

You are with me [1]

When I need a friend that cares - But can't find one   anywhere -

You are with me [2]

You are with me in the night

Walking with me as the light [3]

You are with me through the storm

My heart's freezing - You are warm

You are with me when I cry

Speaking truth when evil lies

When death tells me - love has died [4]

Your love conquers every lie

You are with me [5]

Love lives with me

1. 2 Timothy 2:13
2. Proverbs 18:24
3. John 8:12
4. Song 8:6, Romans 8:37-39, 1 Cor. 15:54,55
5. Job

33

You Chose Me

You chose me - even in my iniquity [1]
You chose me - without any real beauty

You chose me

And in my transgression
You heard my confession [2]
You know my condition
And my destination [3]

You chose me

Your mercy forever enduring
A broken heart repenting [4]

You saw me - You heard me

You love me - You chose me

1. Isaiah 53:5
2. 1 John 1:9
3. Psalm 139
4. Psalm 51:17

Your Peace

Your peace passes all understanding [1]
Your Grace is sufficient for me [2]

Your Love is a love never ending
Your face is the Glory I see

Your presence is always surrounding
Your mercy is new everyday

Your will and your faith are abounding
You draw me to follow your way

Your peace - your grace - your love - your face
I find them all in the secret place [3]

Your peace - your grace - your love - your face
There's nothing on earth that can take their place

1. Philippians 4:7
2. 2 Corinthians 12:9
3. Matthew 6:6

35

You love me

I sleep and You love me
I wake and You love me
I call and You love me
I fall and You love me
I try and You love me
I cry and You love me

I'm hopeless - You love me
I'm faithless - You love me

God, You love me - You formed me
Just as I am

Isaiah 44:21
Jeremiah 31:3
Romans 11:27-9

Chapter Two

Our Love

So I will always love You

You called me out of darkness [1]
Took away all my sadness
Filled my heart with the kindness [2]
Of Your word

You repaired what was broken
Changed the lies that were spoken [3]
Caused my heart to be open - Truth was heard

So I will always love You

I will always love how You reached out for me [4]
I will always love how Your love rescued me [5]
I will always love all You've promised to be [6]
I will always love how Your word kisses me [7]

Light has conquered the darkness [8]

Joy has covered the sadness [9]

My heart's flowing with gladness

With Your word

You repaired what was broken

Changed the lies that were spoken

Caused my heart to be open [10]

Truth was heard

So I will always love You

1. Colossians 1:13, 1 Peter 2:9   2. Psalm 13:5, 31:7

3. Numbers 24:10, Deut. 23:5   4. Romans 5:8

5. John 3;16   6. Deut 4:31

7. Song of Solomon 1:2   8. John 1:5

9. Psalm 30:11 Isaiah 61:3   10. Psalm 27:8

A Living Blessing

I want to be a blessing in this life
For my life is God's Blessing
I want to live a life that speaks of Christ 1

To show the mercy God has given me
So that He receives the Glory
To live by Grace in all sufficiency 2

I want to live the words that I sing
Then His word will be living
So it won't be me but His love people hear
For it's faith that comes by hearing 3
And the hearing by His Word
And by His Spirit, hearts will be restored
Yes, by His Spirit, hearts will be restored [4]

Living through me - Blessing through me
Giving through me - Loving through me
Healing through me - Mercy through me [5]
A living blessing

1. Galatians 2:20   2. 2 Cor. 12:9   3. Romans 10:17
4. Ezekiel 11:19, 36:26, Luke 8:15, John 14:27, 2 Cor. 3:3,
1 Peter 3:4, Galatians 6:1, 1 John 3:20-21
5. Matthew 10:8, Luke 9:2

Morning Song

His mercies are new every morning. One morning I woke up and was doing my daily "thank you Lord" when in my heart I wanted to give Him more. I wanted to praise Him with a   song from my heart, that gives Him the Glory that He deserves. To magnify Him and show my joy and thanks, exuberantly- to have the heart and enthusiasm for God that David had.

In my heart, I felt that a morning song should fill your heart with joy and vitality, and a spirit that jump starts your day.

When you encounter people with this joyous countenance, people will wonder what's going on.

The morning is a good opportunity to share some of the following uplifting words of God with people:

"The joy of the Lord is my strength"   *Nehemiah 8:10*

"The Lord is my Light and my Salvation - whom shall I fear" *Psalm 27:1*

"Thank You Lord, for the joy of Your Salvation" *Psalm 51:12*

"His mercies are new every morning" *Lamentations 3:23*

"He sustains you through the night" *Psalm 55:22*

"He is the morning light - the Light of the world" *John 8:12,   Revelation 22:16*

"He turns your mourning into dancing" *Psalm 30:11*

"Arise and shine for your light has come and the Glory of the Lord has risen on you " *Isaiah 60:1*

The Lord will give all of this freely, to all who ask of Him.
Matthew 7:7, 21:22

Morning Song

I will sing of your love in the morning

For all through the night you sustain me [1]

Each morning you bring your new mercies to me [2]

Your Grace is the light that I see

The birds sing your praise in the morning

Your praise is the first thing I hear

Each morning I lift up this prayer unto you

I pray You will come and draw near

For You are the light

You watch as I sleep [3]

through the night

Your Majesty - Glory - and Power unfold

The sun that the darkness can't hold

You're my delight [4]

With You Lord I walk without fright

Your finest of oils have been poured upon [5]

So I may shine forth like the dawn

I praise you for this morning song

1. Psalm 92:1,2

2. Lamentations 3:21-23

3. Psalm 42:8

4. Psalm 37:4,11

5. Psalm 45:7, 104:15, Isaiah 61:3

Raining on me

I woke up this morning, just thinking of You

Your love covers me, like a soft, morning dew [1]

And it's raining - raining from You

I thought I'd give praise with the radio on

Then I heard You say, would you sing Me a song [2]

So I'm praising- Singing to You

You're my hope for tomorrow - my love for today

Your love keeps on raining and all I can say is

Rain ----------------- Love rain on me [3]

Rain -------------------- All over me

God – You Reign------------and I can see

It's Your love------------- raining on me

Rain on me--------- rain upon me [4]

I love your rain

1. Numbers 11:9
2. Psalm 40:3, 96:1
3. Psalm 133:3
4. Hosea 6:3

43

My first love

I still remember my first love
He came to me like a sweet dove
The life that He gave me
The day that He saved me
I still remember that day
I found new love when I met You
How could I ever forget You
We made a connection
Through Your resurrection [1]
Your love alone - made a way

You're my first love - but You first loved me [2]
I found true love and found a new me
Oh what a love that You gave for me
And You gave -You gave it for free

You have become my first love
All because You first loved me

1. John 11:25

2. Revelation 2:2-4

3. 1 John 4:19

44

Love You More

This song was inspired by Psalm 63:3

His love endures forever - we are living proof of that.
He Loves us with an everlasting love.
Knowing and experiencing this, shouldn't we try to love Him more?
Not more than He loves us, because we cannot achieve that much
love. We need to love Him in a greater capacity, accomplished to
some extent by being more selfless and focused on Him.
We can show our love by trusting more, giving more, serving more
or by being more obedient to His word..
By saying "I love You more than I love my life" you are loving Him
more.

Picture love as a bonding or weaving together of many strands.
When something tries to cut it, the other strands hold it together.
When something pulls on it, the weaving only gets tighter, holding it
together. *Ecclesiastes 4:12.*
If you really love someone, nothing can cut you or pull you apart -
you are with them always.
This is God's love for us : "I Am with you always, even to the end of
the world   *Matthew 28:20*
Nothing can separate us from the love of God.
Romans 8:38,39
Lord, I need to love you more

Love You More

I need to love You more
I need to love You Lord
More than I love my life
I need to love You more

I need to love you Lord
To love You so much more
For Your love is so sure
Your love is greater than life [1]

When I give in to You
Then You give in to me
You lead my heart to see
Your love is part of me

When my love is unsure
You love me even more [2]
My broken heart restored
Because I am adored

I could love my life
Or I could love You Lord
Your love is greater than life
I need to love You more

1. Psalm 63:3
2. 2 Timothy 2:13

Honor my Love

I'm in love with Your Holiness
Your word that comes from above

I'm in love with Your righteousness [1]
That keeps my heart full of love

I'm in love with your Spirit Lord
To guide me as I go Your way

I'm in love with your mercy
You're there when I lose my way

Honor my love - the love that I have for You [2]
Honor my love - the love that comes back to you
Honor my love - Honor my love for You

1. Proverbs 21:21
2. 1 Samuel 2:30, 2 Chronicles1:11-12

I can't stop loving you

I can't stop - loving you
Oh I can't stop - loving you
I can't stop - loving you
No I can't stop - loving you

You can't stop forgiving me
You can't stop setting captives free
Endless love is all I see

So I can't stop loving you
No I can't stop loving you

I can't count all you've done for me
All I know is you've set me free
And you just keep on loving me
So I can't stop loving you
No I can't stop loving you

Endless love is all I see
So I can't stop loving you
No I can't stop loving you

Psalm 103:12

I love You Jesus

I love You Jesus - My Savior Lord
You really paid a price - I could never afford
A final sacrifice - That took all my sin [1]
You opened Heavens door - So I could come in
I love You Jesus

You died upon a cross - You rose from the dead
You truly came to do - All that You said
You are the Lamb of God - The King of Kings
You sit at the Father's Hand - And all Heaven sings
I love You Jesus

My Redeemer - Mighty Savior
You're my lover - You're my friend
You're my Prince of Peace
You're my counselor [2]
You will be with me to the end
I love You Jesus - I love You Jesus

1. Hebrews 9:29, 10:12
2. Isaiah 9:6

49

Love like diamonds

I love you so - Lord, I love you so

You shine like a diamond and you shine upon me [1]

Your love is like diamonds within me

Glory to you God - So precious is your love

So gracious, that you would choose me

Your love has a value, my mind can't conceive

To make me, a mine of your diamonds

Your love within me - brighter than the sun

As bright as the Kingdom that is to come [2]

1. Numbers 6:25

2. Revelation 21:10,11

Song of His Spirit

This song was composed out of this question: "How can I sing a song to you Lord - can my words give you enough love?" I want to both sing and live a love song of spirit and truth to you Lord, from a heart full of love, not just a mouth full of words. Make my life a song to You Lord...

"God is Spirit and those who worship Him must worship in Spirit and in truth." *John 4:24*

We are told in *1 John 3:18* " Let us not love in word or in tongue, but in deed and truth."

I can talk about what I believe until the Lord returns; but if I'm not doing what I believe, how can I make anyone else believe or see the change in me, that came from my salvation through Jesus.

They must see the living testimony of Jesus and want it for themselves. Then they and we, will have a song to sing.. A song of salvation - a song of His Spirit - a real, living, love song.

Song of His Spirit

How can I sing a song to you Lord
What is Your song composed of
When does the music reach Your ears
Can my voice give You enough love

To sing the song You sing for me
We would be in communion
Your Holy Spirit song through me
Oh what a blessed union

So I will sing Your song to You [1]
Sung by Your Spirit within me
Music that Glorifies Your Name
Music to let You draw near me

Songs of salvation - Songs of joy
Songs of the sin that Your Son destroyed [2]
Songs of His light that shines on my face
Songs that are sung in Your Most Holy Place [3]

Let Me hear music - He whispered to me
The music that's played by abiding in Me [4]
Sing this for me - for I sing this for you
Love is the song Jesus sings about you

1. Psalm 40:3
2. Revelation 5:9
3. revelation 15:3
4. 1 John 4:16

You are beautiful

The night is put behind me - As the morning lights the day

A sea of clouds above me - Flowing by like ocean waves

I wake up to this beauty - Knowing God has made it all

I'm covered by Your mercy - And I thank You for it all

You are beautiful - There's none as beautiful as You

You are beautiful - Creation made beautiful by You [1]

The clouds are like brush strokes -

Sweeping softly through the sky

Your wind paints a picture - A picture for your bride

The sun is now rising - And You warm me with the day

You know everything I need [2]

There's no need for me to say

I'll say I love you and You love me

You are beautiful [3]

When I go astray - You love me [4]

You are beautiful - You are here

You're always here - with each new day

This is your way - and it's beautiful

Let me always see - You are beautiful

1. Genesis 1, Ecclesiastes 3:11,   2. Matthew 6:31-32

3. Psalm 48:1,2,   4. 2 Timothy 2:13

You're Easy to Love

God, You're so easy to love
You reign over me from above
Your peace is the song of a dove
You're easy to love
As I sleep, You rejoice over me [1]
I just wake up and breathe and receive
Keep my heart fixed on You and believe
You're easy to love
I love You because You first loved me [2]
And You've made it so easy to see
You love me and You've made me to be
Easy to love
I am weak, when I want to be strong
And You still sing to me Your love song
When I cry You will capture my tears [3]
When I'm lost, I have found You are near [4]
You're easy to love
You're easy to love because You've first loved me
Easy to love and so easy to see
You love me and You've made me to be
Easy to love

1. Zephaniah 3:17   2. 1 John 4:19
3. Ps 56:8, 126:5   4. Psalm 34:18

55

My love is your love

There is no love without You
For love is all about You
Without it I'd be hopeless
In a world that's loveless

I must come to you for love
For Your love has come to me
You make it plain to see
My love is Your love

John 13:36:37

Chapter Three

Intimacy

Intimacy with God

Intimacy with God, is a time when you get close to and experience the love of God, in a personal way. A time when it's just you and Him, when you devote your time and desire to only being close to Him. It's a time when he speaks to your spirit about you - not someone or something else. He touches you where you need to be touched by Him. Intimate times can enhance your joy, your love, your humility, compassion, sympathy, your worship, health, faith, your discernment, your feelings of mercy or forgiveness. He will make you more like Him and more in love with Him, in your intimate times. These times are for you alone. No one else would understand how God is touching you, because it's just for you. Group intimacy isn't like one on one. He will be intimate with us as a group, so we may share intimacy with each other, but we need to be one on one, to enhance our own relationship with Him.

I've had intimate times with the Lord that I've shared with people, who just didn't get it.

Later on, as I thought about it, I felt like I had shared private information with someone.

Feeling convicted in my spirit and sort of embarrassed, I had to ask God to forgive me, for sharing what He wanted only me to have. I really felt like I had lessened what God had shown or told me. Some of my most intimate times have been when I didn't approach Him but when he had something for me and surprised me, calling me to be with Him right then and there.

Times like these, really build your faith and your love and awareness that He is wanting to spend time with you, not just when you're ready. His love for you is already the ultimate intimacy and is available all of the time. Be ready to reach out and hold on to Him when He calls.

My Sister my Bride

My sister my Bride - come stand here beside me

Come and be my Bride

My sister my Bride - come walk along with me

Stay with me by My side

For I love you - yes I love you

I love you - My sister my Bride

How I love you - yes I love you - I love you

My sister My Bride

I'll nurture your heart - with My grace and loving

My love keeps your heart warm

When your heart's in need - I'm always there giving

I will keep you from harm

For I love you - yes I love you - I love you

My sister my Bride

How I love you - yes I love you

I want you here by my side

You are My sister My Bride

Solomon 4:9-12, Revelation 21:2

Psalm 23eed

I'm glad to be guided by the Shepherd
To pastures that are green
Resting by the waters - the waters cool and clean
Sitting at His table - in the face of trouble
The enemy may rob me but my God returns me double [1]
His rod and staff bring comfort -
my soul is saved from wrath
He says His ways are righteous - so I'll walk upon His path

Oil permeates my head - His fragrance on my breath [2]
Evil cannot touch me in the valley veiled by death
His goodness and His mercy are with me through my strife [3]
On my journey to His house - filled with eternal life

The Lord is my Shepherd - what more do I need
My prayers have been honored - I am Psalm 23eed

Psalm 23eed - what more do I need
Resting by the waters - the waters cool and clean
Psalm 23eed - evil can't touch me
I walk through the valley with the Shepherd guiding me
Yes I am Psalm 23eed

1. Isaiah 61:7, Job 42:10 .2. Revelation 5:8, 8:4. 3. Psalm 116:1

61

Returning to Your love

I keep returning - I keep returning to You [1]

My heart is burning - My heart is yearning for You

I have a passion - It's a reaction to You

You are my attraction - my satisfaction is You

There's no other like You I could find

Until I could see You - I was blind

I choose my way sometimes - but it's rough

So I keep returning to Your love

Yes I keep returning to Your love

Isaiah 44:22   Jeremiah 24:7

When I think about the Lord

When I think about the Lord and all that He has done

When I think of all I've lost and all that He has won [1]

I can only stand amazed - when I think about the Lord

When I think about the Lord and His amazing grace [2]

And the Light of the world that shines on my face [3]

I can only stand amazed-when I think about the Lord

I am so amazed - at the love He has for me

So amazed at what He sees in me [4]

Amazed that He'd do this all for me

Amazed - I'm so amazed

Amazed - when I gaze into His face

Amazed and I'm in a Holy place

Amazed that I'm welcome to abide [5]

In His heart - where I can hide

I'm so amazed

When I think about the Lord [6]

I stand amazed

When I think about the Lord

1. Romans 5:8
2. 2 Corinthians 12:9
3. John 8:12
4. Matthew 26:34, 74,75
5. 1 John 4:13
6. James 3:12

63

Where You are

When I open up my eyes - You are there
When I open up your word - You are there
When I open up my life - You are there
When I open up my heart - You are there [1]

I want to be where You are

I look to the Heavens - and I see where You are
Though You're in the Heavens
You're closer than the stars

Creation's song is over [2]
Though the music is still here
And it lingers so near
Your song is within me [3]

That's where You are

1. Psalm 139:8
2. Genesis 2;1-3
3. Psalm 40:3

Closer to you

What can I do to be closer to you
To give you my love and to just adore you [1]
I adore you

Where must I be, so you stand beside me
Where I open my eyes and it's you that I see [2]
Just to see you
To be near you - Closer to you

Closer than a brother [3]
With a love like no other
You said you'd never go
I must be closer than I know
Closer to you

1. James 4:8, 2 Cor. 5:8
2. Hebrews 7:19
3. Proverbs 18:24

Dear Jesus

You love me more than I know

You have a love for me that is hidden from my view

My eyes could not endure its intensity

But I feel it - the enormity of it around me

I never want to only imagine your love

My imagination can't match your love

Just surround me - live in me and through me

And I'll feel the power of your love within me

You are much more than a visual experience

And more than my senses can comprehend

You are why my heart beats - why my lungs breathe

Why I sleep and dream and awaken every day

When I express this love for me - other's will see it

They will know and want your love for them

Your love for me is even greater than my expectations

Of your love for me

I don't expect that anyone can do what only you can

Dear Jesus, I love you

John 17

Desperate for You

If I'm desperate for anything - I'm desperate for You

Tried almost everything - there's no one like you

The world is uncertain but Jesus you're still the same [1]

You first loved me - that's why I love You

You guard my heart and guide me to you

You are my Shepherd - You keep me from wandering [2]

So I'm desperate - I'm desperate for you

Yes I'm desperate - I'm desperate for You

Help me to never forget my first love [3]

Let me remember your grace is enough

Nothing I do can compare to the things you've done

I'm desperate - I'm desperate for you

Oh Jesus - I'm calling for you

If there's one thing that's certain - It's you've set me free

You walk beside me and never leave me

No way I'm falling, while your love is holding me

I still remember - when I first met You

There in your Glory - I bowed before you

My heart was aching - and You came to comfort me

So I'm desperate - I'm desperate for you

Oh Jesus - I'm desperate for you

1. Hebrews 13:8
2. John 10:3-5
3. Revelation 2:4,7

67

Intimacy

Hearing from God

Can you hear God? He may not talk to you to your face, or tell you what you want to hear. Though if you listen, you will hear Him through the media that He chooses. It may be situational, people, movies, dreams, songs - God loves songs. He will tell you what you need to hear through a song.

A few years ago, I was in the process of remodeling a house. A week or so before, I had lost my hammer and couldn't find it. I was using a hammer that belonged to the owner of the house I was working on, to do some other work. When I returned to the house, I took his hammer back in with me and wondered to myself: "Where is my hammer?"

My work for the day was in the kitchen, so I turned on the radio and started to work on the cabinets. Thinking about my hammer again, since I needed it and really liked the feel of it, I opened up an upper cabinet door and there was my hammer, lying in the cabinet. I said out loud: "Hey, there's my hammer!" The music was playing and the instant I grabbed the hammer, I heard the singer on the radio sing these words; "The hand on the hammer was God's."

The song continued and I stood there with this hammer in my hand. A wave of energy went right through my body, from head to toe. I was struck in my spirit by the depth of the words to this song that I've never heard before.

The Holy Spirit upon me was overwhelming and this feeling of joy and the love of God came over me, as I stood there, gazing at my hammer. What an awesome presence this was.

I could feel the presence of God with me in that kitchen. Then amazingly, the next two or three songs were some of my favorites, so I just stopped working and was singing along, worshiping God, with a hammer in my hand.

I was set up - God had something to tell me and He used a hammer and a song on the radio to do it. He was telling me that He loves me - that He uses hammers for building Kingdoms - that I was not guilty. This was His chosen time to be intimate with me.

He could be speaking to you right now, as you're reading this- do you hear Him? He hears you, He wants you to hear Him - every day and He will hear your call - He loves you.

Sensitivity leads to intimacy.

Here in my heart

Jesus direct me - guide and protect me
Jesus be Lord of my life [1]
Jesus reveal me - show me what's in me
Help me to make my life right [2]
Jesus adore me - come and restore me
I want to walk in Your light
I am believing - that You will be loving
Forever be loving me [3]
My heart is yearning - to see your returning
To be in eternity
You won't forsake me - You said You will take me
So I'm waiting here patiently [4]
Here in my heart - Speak to me tenderly
Here in my heart - I want your love to be
Here in my heart
I want Your love to be here
Here in my heart - I want the world to see
Here in my heart - You are alive in me [5]
Here in my heart
Waiting for You to draw near [6]
Here in my heart

1. John 10:27,   2. Psalm 51
3. Jeremiah 31:3
4. Isaiah 40:31   5. I John 4:16   6. James 4:8

70

HERE

Reaching into empty silence
Searching for your Holy presence
Trying to draw near
Working through my own resistance
Moving past the walls of darkness
Knowing light is near
Draw me with your loving kindness
Take away all of my blindness
So I can see clear –So I see you here
Sensing all your loving kindness
Touched by love in all forgiveness
All you freely give
Grace is flowing like a river
And the mercies you deliver
Let your spirit live
Reaching into all your fullness
Finding you are in my presence
Knowing you are here
Now I offer no resistance
Light has covered all the darkness
Now I know you're here
You have been my loving kindness
Took away all of my blindness
Now I can see clear - Now I see you here

Matthew 28:20

71

Love is part of you

The love of God abides in you, when you acknowledge His love. You house His love within you. When you don't feel loved by others, you can go within yourself and dwell with the love of God that is always within you and find your love and peace with His love.

Even if you were like me, thinking that you have no love for life or for God, and life seems hopeless. You still have an in-born level of love within you. There is always just enough love within you to draw you near to God. He is always there with you, even if you are not with Him.

When everything else has fallen away - when the walls fall down and the heart opens up, that's when love draws near. Desperation and desire, draw His love and joy creates love. Forgiveness, giving and receiving, provoke love. We did not create these actions on our own.

They are part of us - a part of God within us, necessary to bring about His love.

We should all make an effort to cultivate love, through all of the emotions and circumstances of this life.

The answer is You

I've been wandering - I've been away from you
My faith has been fleeting
You are forgiving - Your mercy still flows from you [1]
The only answer is You
Keep me in your will - Help me to be still
In your love
Staying with you - returning to my first love
For You first loved me

You are faithful to light my way
Forgiving me - restoring me
Whatever the question
The answer is You [2]

1. 2 Timothy 2:13
2. Psalm 119:1- 176

Holy Kiss

Kiss me with a Holy kiss
Let me feel you on my face [1]
There is no greater love than this
Knowing we are face to face [2]
May your words caress my ears
Your compassion dry my tears
Your words will restore my soul [3]
A Holy kiss can touch the soul
Kiss me with a Holy kiss
My soul is longing for the bliss

1. Song of Solomon 1:12, Romans 16:16, 1Peter 5:14
2. Genesis 33:11, Hebrews 4:12
3. Isaiah 38:17, Psalm 23:3

I am my Beloved's

I am my beloved's - my beloved is mine [1]

He has been my lover since before I knew time [2]

I can call upon Him and He listens to me [3]

I will be there with Him when my time here is done

I will be there with Him

I will be there with Him when my time here is done [4]

I am my beloved's - my beloved is mine

1. Song of Solomon 6:3, 7:10
2. John 17:24
3. Psalm 17:6, 18:6
4. Matthew 25:34

I hear You

I hear You in the falling rain

I hear You in the wind [1]

You are heard in everything [2]

I know I'll hear You again [3]

In the wind - in the rain

In my joy - in my pain

Let Your mercy fall like rain [4]

Shower down Your love again

So I hear You

1. Job 28:25
2. Isaiah 55:12, Romans 8:23
3. Numbers 12:6
4. Hosea 6:3

I'm trying to love

I'm trying to love
I'm crying to love
The path I'm on has me struggling and falling
I need your hand of love
Lord, Hear me calling
Catch my tears in your hand
Be my shepherd - be my Lord
Hear my cry - my cry for life

I'm crying for the world [1]
I'm crying to you Lord
Take my tears of sorrow
Make them tears of joy

I'm crying and calling
I'm trying and falling
Hear me Lord
Help me Lord
Love me Lord
I'm trying to love

1. Habakkuk 1:2-4, Jonah 3:9, 4:2,10,11

Intimacy

I love you

If I said to you: "I love you" - would you believe me?
Your reply might be, that I don't even know you- how could I
 love you? True, we don't know each other but I have a Godly
 love for you and you can possess the same for me or anyone else.
Godly love is a love for life - not just your own.
Empathy, sympathy, compassion, serving and self - sacrifices
emulate Godly love.
Realize what you are committing yourself to, when you say
to someone: "I love you."
In essence you are saying: "I want you to breathe - I want you to live
and breathe the same air with me."

When you take your last breath, it will also be your first   breath
of a new life called eternity. In eternity, you'll be living in the breath
of God - the breath that spoke creation into being.
You'll be living in love itself - living in "I love you."

In your love

I've been away from you - I've been near to you
My faith has been fleeting - You are forgiving
Your mercy still flows from you
The only answer is you

Keep me in your will - help me to be still
In your love
Staying with you - with my first love
You first loved me - in your love

1 John 4

Infinite Love

We are destined for eternity
In God's infinite love
His mercy endures forever [1]

What a beautiful, infinite vision
A picture without a border
A song you always hear
A memory that never leaves you
A love that is always near

Infinity - there but here - forever [2]
We'll always be held together
With Infinite love

1. Isaiah 54:8
2. Luke 23:43

80

Inhabit me

Inhabit me - Make your habitation in me

You inhabit the praises of your people [1]

I praise you Lord - inhabit me

As the stars inhabit the sky - inhabit me

The earth is yours and all its fullness

Inhabit me

Holy spirit fill this place - take away all my disgrace

Make your habitation in me [2]

Love of God - abide in me - inhabit me

1. Psalm 22:3

2. Psalm 26:8,33:14, 2 Corinthians 5:2, Ephesians 2:22

Into Your Heart

You took me out of my head and into Your heart
The day that I said – I need a new start [1]
Out of my head and into Your heart
You took away all the things - I don't understand [2]
And showed me You hold them all in Your hand
Out of my head and into Your heart

Though my heart was in doubt -Your love is so great [3]
You turned me around - Your love doesn't wait
Out of my head and into Your heart

Your peace passes all understanding [4]
Took away all my heart was demanding
You speak from spirit to spirit [5]
My heart is letting me hear it
Out of my head and into Your heart

1. Romans 10:9
2. Isaiah 55:7-9, Romans 12:2
3. 1 John 3:19-21
4. Philippians 4:7
5. John 6:63, 14:26, 15:26, Acts 2:4, 20:22, 1 Cor. 12:8, ,14:2,
Revelation 2:7

Just a Glimpse of You

Just a glimpse of You and I'd be renewed [1]

What my heart would do at the sight of You

Just a glimpse of You

Just to see Your Face - in this Holy Place

Just a glimpse of You

What my heart would do at the sight of You

Just a glimpse of You

Job 23:9,10, Psalm 17:15,80:3

Let me be with You this way

"Is it about me or about Him?"

I had been walking with the Lord for several years. One day, I simply became lost in myself and questioned where my walk was getting me. I had been to every Church service I could attend and read scores of articles by the most anointed writers and speakers. There were prayer meetings, educational classes, where they give you a certificate of completion to put on your wall, but I didn't feel complete.

(*2 Cor. 3:1*) I even had a name badge to put on my chest, but I knew who I was.

In my search to be found, I served in every area of the Church. All that I found though, was that I was still lost. My focus was on me and what everyone thought about me, not on who God already knew that I was. Many of us have been there - some of us are now.

There I was, a fruit tree with a tag on it but no fruit. People need to see fruit to know what kind of tree you are. They don't need a certificate or a name badge to tell them.

(2 Cor. 4:2) Fruit speaks for itself.

So I prayed to God, to ask what it was that I wasn't doing. I sat alone in my room and talked with Him. "What do I have to do?" I asked. I heard in my spirit: "You are now doing what I want you to do". "What is that ?" I asked. It was then that I heard in my heart: "Nothing"- "Nothing but my Grace for you". Our awards or people's approval of them, do not put the focus on God - they put it on you. (*Galatians1:10*)

Some people try to make you focus on their focus on you, which actually puts their focus on themselves. Evidently a lot of people are walking around out of focus - running into everything but God.

When my focus is on me and not on God, I am self-satisfied or maybe even self-sabotaging myself. This happens when I think I can build something better than He has already built Himself. When I do nothing but ask for His guidance, I have His Grace and He has my attention.

I am then able to receive all that He has for me. "His Grace is greater than anything we can or cannot do: *Isaiah 45:1-13* "Absence from the flesh is presence with God." *(2 Cor. 5:8)*

Realizing this, my focus had changed. The following Wednesday evening at church, the worship music started to play and play, soft consuming music. The sweet presence of God was honoring our worship and praise to Him. As I sat in this peaceful state, as much as I love to sing, I just couldn't sing anymore. The next words out of my mouth were these: "Let me be with You this way". The rest of the words flowed from deep within my spirit, as I was inspired by this intimate experience, to write this song...

What strikes me as odd, is that the words to this song or prayer, are about being quiet. Read the words but absorb the spirit of the message. God speaks to us, Spirit to Spirit, when we are quiet in His Presence. If you don't hear a thing or speak a word, you are in the right place to hear, Spirit to spirit.

His desire is to be with you this way....

Let me be with You this way

Let me be with You this way
With no words I have to say [1]
Let me stay with You right here
Where Your Spirit is so near

There's a peace surrounding me
As Your presence abounds me
Nothing else can cloud my mind
No resistance I can find

I would stay with You forever
By the stillness of Your water [2]
In the fullness of Your Grace
In this restful - Holy place

Let me be with You this way
Where my thoughts have gone away
With no words I have to say
Let me be with You, I pray

1. 2 Chronicles 2:13-14
2. Psalm 23:2

Lord, I want You

I want a new revelation from You

Not just my imagination of You [1]

I want to hear You so clearly

That I feel You near me

To be in relation with You [2]

So kiss me with a Holy kiss

Let me feel You on my face

There's no greater love than this

Knowing we are face to face [3]

1. Genesis 8:12, Romans 1:21, Colossians 2:8

2. 1 Chronicles 2:18

3. Exodus 33:11, 1 Cor. 13:12

Like a Dove

Lord I love your ways
Yes I love your ways [1]
So I'll seek your face
In a secret place [2]
Lord I love your ways

And I'll fly away - like a dove - away [3]
To a secret place
Where I'll see your face
Yes I'll hide away - I will hide away
In that secret place - with you - face to face [4]

Lord I love your ways
Yes I love your ways

1. Psalm 119:1-15
2. Matthew 6:6,18
3. Psalm 55:6, Isaiah 38:14
4. 1 Corinthians 13:12

Lord I want your touch

Lord , I want to hear you

Have you heard through me

Lord, I want to see you

So you are seen in me

Lord, I want to touch you

Feel your love within me

Touching me

Freeing me - from me

Lord, I want your touch

Psalm 51, 55:12,13 - 119:133

Love's mystery

As I look into the sky so blue
I see an image formed by You
It's such a Glorious canopy [1]
Your love that always covers me [2]

You're so open to what is me
That is such a mystery
And the heavens are clear
So that I may draw near

Not a cloud in the sky
Now it's just You and I
Then as one whispers by
We have met eye to eye

It's love's mystery [3]
Your love for me

1. Isaiah 4:5,6
2. Psalm 27:5
3. 1 Cor. 15:51, Colossians 1:27

More like You

It's not what I did
But what You will do
It's not about me
But all about You

I don't define me
And You remind me
That as You refine me
I'll be more like You

Malachi 3:2-4

Only You

The works of my flesh displease you [1]
The lusts of my eyes offend you
My desire is to only love you
Why do my thoughts turn from you [2]

My first love should be only you [3]
My only gaze should be upon you
No other god should be before you [4]
No other god can do what you do

You are my God - I'll have no other
I'll no longer fall to the lies of another
You are my God - So I won't turn away
You are my God - the truth and the way

I will pursue you with passion
And you will draw near to me [5.]
You reach out with compassion
Only You can reach me

1. Psalm 51:1-4   2. James 1:8
3. Revelation 2:4
4. Exodus 20:3, Leviticus 26:1
5. James 4:8

Senses of Your love

I want to feel your love -
Like your hand on my head [1]
I want to hear your love -
In the words that you've said [2]

I want to smell your love - like a Holy perfume [3]
Taste your love - like a garden in bloom
I want to see my King - walking into my room [4]

1. Psalm 23:5, 1 Samuel 16:13
2. Song of Solomon 1:12
3. Song of Solomon 3:4
4. Isaiah 59:21

93

Soaking in Your love

Soaking in the stream of Your love

Soaking in a stream from above [1]

Drenched by Your presence - praising your name

Never leaving thirsty - never the same - never the same

Drinking in the love that You give

Filling up my spirit within

I'm overflowing - flowing with You

The stream that is flowing- flowing from You -

Only from You

Soaking in Your love

Drinking in Your love

Flowing in Your love

The River of Your love [2]

I'm overflowing - flowing with you

The river is flowing - flowing from you

Flowing from you [3]

Only from You – only from You

Resting in Your love

Living in Your love

Soaking in Your love

The River of Your love

1. Psalm 46:4
2 .Jeremiah 17:7,8
3. Ezekiel 47:9

94

You in Me

Feeling tired and weary as I wrote this verse - reminiscing   about my childhood days and the things I wished were different. Feeling drained and not knowing what to pray, as I lie in my bed. I started to say the "Now I lay me down to sleep" prayer. In my soul I was a bit distressed, in my flesh I was longing for sleep, in my mind, I was dwelling on things I didn't need to be . The past can't be changed. In my spirit, where the Lord lives, I realized I was at peace and that all is well with Him in me.
I knew that He knows how I'm feeling. I knew my trust was in Him. I knew He is always with me. Just thinking about Him and my faith in Him, changed my whole countenance, and I thought: "You are my reward, for the faith and trust I have in You. " When every part of me has been downcast, Your spirit still lives in me. You are the lifter of my head. If ever I have lost my sense of self- worth, You remind me by Your Spirit , that You are my reward..

I thank You Lord..

You in me

I trust You Lord to hold my heart

Your Word says we will never part

In You alone I put my trust

With you alone can my soul rest [1]

You know me Lord and all I say

All my thoughts and all I pray [2]

Hear my heart - Oh hear me Lord

You in me - is my reward

You in me - is my reward [3]

1. Psalm 62:1, 66:16

2. Psalm 139:1-5

3. Colossians 1:27

Chapter Four

Exhortations

The Tree and the serpent

In the Garden, a serpent spoke to Eve about the fruit on a tree. She listened to his lies about why and what she should eat, which distracted her from the truth that God had spoken. God said not to eat from the tree that the serpent was speaking of - the tree of the knowledge of good and evil. Look at the condition of our world. We all live in one big battle over what is good and what is evil - what's right and what's wrong. We even make our own rules now, to accommodate our appetites. Don't swallow what the enemy feeds you. Let the truth of God's word nourish you.

The following is my dream of the tree and the serpent and how it pertains to this book.

Soon after I gave my life to the Lord, I had a dream. I was standing at the edge of a large forest. There, a woman was sitting in one of the trees. Beside her was a dead snake, hanging over the branch. As I looked beyond her, there were dead snakes hanging over branches in all of the trees. I asked her what all of these snakes were.

She said to me: "This is the enemy you have just defeated- the rest of these are the enemies that you will defeat in the future." I had no idea what was in store for me - defeating all of these enemies. I had quite a few battles, until the day that I realized that they were already defeated - in reality as well as in the Heavenly realm. I have won every battle, up to this point and I believe that in faith, I have won every battle that is to come. It's not "warfare" - it's faith.

We are "Surrounded by His love" not by enemies.

You may be wondering what a dream about snakes in trees has to do with a book about love.

I was also wondering, as I was writing. I heard in my spirit, that there are many breeds of snakes, or lies and temptations, and many types of trees or people. God has given me various approaches with my writings, for each type or level of understanding, concerning these snakes.

Our rationalizations, pride or knowledge do not defeat the enemy. Love and forgiveness and the word of God defeated the enemy (1 Corinthians 8:1-3)

They are the spiritual forces that repel the enemy of our souls, just as worship and praise do.

I believe that each of us are one of those trees in that forest and that one or more of the writings in this book, speaks of how the snake in your tree was or will be defeated, therefore giving you confirmation and or encouragement concerning My hope and prayer is that you'll find it in this book and maybe recognize someone else's tree and show them how love has defeated their serpent. Don't let this talk about snakes turn you off. Consider this scenario: You're in the desert, parched- hungry- tired, and the snake that you fear, approaches you.

The object of your fear has just become a remedy for it. In your hunger and weariness, you realize that the poisonous serpent who tempts you and seeks to take your life, is now a source of life. You're no longer afraid but empowered and you seize the opportunity to sustain your life, by overcoming that which is trying to take it. When the enemy sees that you realize this, he turns and runs from you. You don't have to eat him, he just has to know that you know you can.

By receiving the spirit and truth of God, that He alone will feed you - you reject the enemy. Recognize this as a lesson from a wilderness experience. God feeds us in the wilderness. Yes, God will even use the enemy to feed you and make you stronger and victorious.

Your finding victory in this book, will make this dream of victory over the serpents in the trees a reality -giving all the glory due to God, who makes our dreams come true.

Life in the wilderness

The enemy tries to feed you lies in the wilderness. He will tell you that you're hungry, tell you that you have nothing, tell you to make your own bread, tell you to end your life because there is no hope, no friends, no spouse, no God. He will tell you that he is god and to follow him.
(*Matthew 4:1-4*)
He will lead you into an abyss and leave you there. He wants to end your life in the wilderness, before you can hear God. He knows that the wilderness is where you will hear God, like no other place, because there is nothing there but God.

Most of us have been in the wilderness. Many of us have avoided God directing us there. I have. I thought it was the enemy. Would you willfully go there?
Don't ever blame the enemy for your being there - though you may meet him there.
Are you tired of confronting the enemy - waiting to confront God?
Do you want to experience God in a deeper way and retain it indefinitely?
Consider the wilderness experience, don't avoid it or regret it. You will find yourself thanking God for it.

Yearning and learning - that's the wilderness.

Some of the most amazing acts of God were born through people who have come from there. It's a place of challenges to find God, to be obedient or to know Him more. Abraham, Moses, Joseph, Elijah, Job, David, Esther, Ruth, Mary, Jesus, John and Paul were all there. (*Mark 6: 31-42*)

You may have been there and didn't recognize it and came out more victorious than you know.

You came out sandy, dry, thirsty and hungry, but with a new awareness and a deeper appreciation and love for what's outside of the wilderness and for God. He was waiting for you there - though He was always with you, all the way through the wilderness. That may be what you were missing. There is life in the wilderness. God will put you where ever it takes for you to find Him and find life - not just in a church or in a ministry or in comfortable surroundings. The wilderness breeds Holiness.

God - You are Poetry

The balance of Your creation is poetry

Time and Your word are rhyme and harmony

I don't have to write it - I can see, hear, smell it
Touch the poetry of His creation

He is within you - poetry
The Sun lighting the day
The voice and the song [1]

The words on a page
The kiss of two lovers
Wind through the trees

The dew on the ground in the morning

His Holy Spirit among us is poetry

His love for you is poetry

God - You are poetry [2]

1. 1 Samuel 10:5
2. Psalm 57:8

My prayer to the Lord
(paraphrasing the Lord's prayer)

God You are my Father in Heaven

You are Holy and glorified

Your Kingdom is coming

Your will is being done

Here on Earth

As we appeal to Heaven

You give us our bread daily

You have forgiven and continue

To forgive our sins

And we must forgive others sins

You provide a way out of temptation

That delivers us from the ways of evil

Your ways are of the Kingdom of Heaven

All power belongs to You

And all of the Glory is Yours

For all eternity

This I believe

Matthew 6:9

Your first lover

You don't need another lover
Just remember your first lover [1]
Stay with one who's there forever

Don't go searching deep inside
He is right there by your side
Feel His touch - He's holding you

You're the one He loves

Don't forget your first love
The songs of love you're singing
He's the lover in the words
The words from the beginning [2]

You don't need another lover
Just remember your first lover

1. 1 John 4:19
2. Genesis 1:29-31

When love calls to you

What do you do - when love calls to you

Follow only a love that follows you

A love that doesn't charge a price

Or ask you for a sacrifice

That sacrifice was already made [1]

And the price was already paid [2]

It's a love that you will never find

With the imagination of your mind

Follow a love that follows you

When you hear love call to you [3]

1. Hebrews 10:12, 1John 4:10
2. 1 Corinthians 6:19,20
3. John 10:11-14

To sing a new love song

I'm the spirit of the music - I'm the spirit of the song
I live within you - so you sing along [1]

I'll give the words to you
So I can sing through you

So allow me to use you
To sing a new love song

1. Psalm 40:3, 98:1

107

Love the world

I'm in the world - not of it [1]
And I'm told that I must love it [2]
I see people never changing
And their hearts need re-arranging
I try to really love them
Without hovering above them [3]
So I'll love the world - Yes I'll love the world
Be a light in darkest places
Shine a light on weary faces [4]
Yes I'll love the world

All I can do is love them
And pray to God above them
For He so loved the world
How could I not love the world
So I'll love the world - Yes I'll love the world

1. John 17:16, Romans 12:2
2. Matthew 6:14,15, 1 John 4:20
3.Matthew 6:1-5, James 4:6
4 .Luke 1:79, Romans 2:19, Acts 26:18, 1Peter2:9

Love is God

God created love

Not idols for us to kill each other over

We created them - He told us not to

God created us to love Him - to love each other

Don't put a name on your love for God

The name of God deserves all the Glory

Don't try to make people love your idols

Love people with the love that God put within you

There is only one love - The Lord God is One

God united us - idols divide us

These idols all want to be number one

Not one of them are

Keep yourself from idols

1 John 5:21

The News Today

I was looking - at the news today

So many have the blues today

With rape and theft and hate and war

Don't let children suffer - no - no more

If we don't soon stop all this madness

We'll be lost in sorrow - Bye-Bye gladness

I saw it in the news today

But it doesn't have to be this way

One way to change the print on that paper

We have to learn to love one another

Just lift your voice to God and pray

For this shame and sorrow to go away

It can happen if we all pray together

If we don't - things may never ever get better

With faith and trust and love so pure

Doing things that God so adores

The News today

Pray for peace in the news today

Lift your voice to God and pray

Peace - God - please

Peace - God - please

No more - don't let children suffer

Learn to love - love one another

We can change - the print on that paper

I want to see peace - in the news, today

I want to see hope - in the news, today

I want to see love - in the news, today

I want to read about it, every day

Learn to love - learn to love - love one another

Extra ! Extra! Read all about it!

God is alive! He lives in you!

John 13:34

Love and Forgiveness

Of all the omnipotent power that God possesses,
He chose love and forgiveness as the most powerful tools to
defeat the enemy.

Choose love and forgiveness and watch the enemy run.

Live a Godly life

That's love - that's forgiveness

As God has forgiven you - forgive others

1 John 4: 7-8

Love is more than a word

What is love? Who has it right- everyone ? We hear: "God is love" - we say: "I love you" You say: "I love ice cream" - I say: "I love that song." Love is a word with so much power. The word can be almost hypnotic or apparently time stopping, in some circumstances.

The word love, has the power to win someone's heart forever, the power to entice someone to give you a gift , the power to heal, the power to spare you punishment for doing something wrong, the power to send someone into a burning building, the power to get you out of trouble with your spouse. Love had the power to have someone die for our sins.

I find it quite amazing, that just the word can silence a room, changing the atmosphere.

Love can stop an argument or start one, make you laugh or cry or both. Saying it to a loved one who has passed on to Glory can bring you peace by believing in your heart that they hear you.

Love is an amazing word, but most effective as a verb - in that there are much better results in living the word than just saying it. Love is more than a word that tickles the ear.

Love makes the greatest distance seem so near.

What a word, love is.

Let love live

God loves us so much that he loves us through people

And he loves people through us

The next time you need to feel God's love

Love a person near you

Let them feel God's love through you

You'll feel God's love, through your love for them

Let love live

Whether you are receiving or giving

Love is there living

1 John 4:7-11

Reconciliation A chord of love

Draw them back to you with your fragrance

Let them seek your face and your presence

May I be the fragrance of You

To draw all people to you

Make my life with you - like a fragrance [1]

And the rhyme of a song verse

That they'll hear and sing out to you

Like a chord of love - sung with you

Reconcile us Lord - all together [2]

Reconciled to you - and forever

Like a chord of love - harmonizing

Music of the Lord - hear it rising

Like a chord of love - reconciling

1 .Ephesians 5:2

2. 2 Corinthians 5:18

I love the Jesus in you

When I see you praying for somebody new

Reaching your hands out and holding them too

Sharing the loving that Jesus gave you

I see the Jesus in you

When I see the Jesus in you that I know

Not seeking approval or making a show [1]

Loving and serving and teaching His word

I know it's Jesus I've heard

I love the Jesus in you

I love the life He gives through you

When you don't claim the things you do

Jesus is living inside of you

Laughing and crying and Dancing around

Playing like children until we fall down

Singing so freely that Heaven can hear [2]

Jesus is standing so near

Go ahead and prophesy if that's what you do

Speak in new voices when they come to you [3]

Don't be discouraged if they don't come through

Just try to let Jesus shine through [4]

1. Galatians 1:10, 2:20.   2. Matthew 18:1-6.   3. 1 Cor. 13:2. 14:1,5,25,26.
4. Revelations 19:10

116

Holiness - A love song within you

When the music is over - His song is still here [1]

If you listen, you'll hear it - the song of His spirit

The music that lingers so near [2]

He is here through us - for He lives within us [3]

Let Holiness come forth from you

Like a love song within you

That can't live without you

The song of His spirit in you [4]

1. 2 Chronicles 5:13,14
2. Revelation 4:8
3. Galatians 2:20, 1 Timothy 1:16
4. Psalm 108:1

He is the Holy One

Would you ever wear a crown of thorns

Let them beat you until you're torn

None but God could last so long

Would you die for one who did you wrong

Would you do it for someone else

Would you do it to save yourself [1]

Don't try to save me, it's already done

We needed a Savior - God sent us His Son

He came here to do - What we couldn't do

He did it for me - He did it for you [2]

Don't try to save me, it's already done

He is the Holy One

The One who cried out "It is done!"

We are the forgiven ones

We are all the Father's sons [3]

He is the Holy One

His love saved us all

1. Matthew 20:18-22
2. Hebrews 10:10
3. Luke 20:36, John 1:12

118

God says love

Leaders be leaders - Men be men
Women and children come first
God says : " Love"
Leaders, act upon the wrong - now
Stop immorality - stop perversion
God says: "Love"
When the world deceives you and denies you
When they say your are hopeless
God says : " Love"
Returning the hearts of the fathers to the children
And the hearts of the children to the fathers
Should flow from the leaders on down
Someone needs to stand in the gap
God says : " Love"
Children are being sold and they pay the price
Paying with their own body, soul and mind
Some for the lusts of their own fathers
God says : " Love"

Fathers - save the children

Malachi 4

119

Love and Fear

Love and forgiveness are more effective tools than fear or judging or placing penalties.

Love has compassion, empathy and sympathy - love never shows apathy. Love is a forgiver - a finder and a keeper. Love is no secret. True love lives within you, it comes from the depth of you. Beware of false love, it's easy to uncover. Having no endurance or perseverance, its motivation is usually to fulfill a need of its own. You can spot superficial love. It's usually focused on itself or making an idol of

itself, doing nothing that models Godly love. Such a love is only self-love and will ultimately have no love for you.

Fear needs love to find healing. Perfect love will cast out fear. (*1 John 4:18*)

If you find yourself in fear of love, it's not love that you fear. It's probably someone who is using fear adversely, to feed their own self-interest or what they can get from you, under the guise of love. True love will never confront you with fear. Should someone try to gain your love through fear - walk away. Follow your heart, where God directs His love.

Don't let yourself be scared into loving someone - let them love you into loving them.

Love is patient and kind - fear is in a hurry and selfish.

Love will allow you to make calm decisions.

Love takes care of love.

Freedom to love

There will be love - There will be hope
There will be joy - There will be peace
And freedom [1]

There is a time - There is a place
There is a day - You'll see His face
And freedom

Freedom from pain - Freedom from sin
Freedom from blame - Free to begin
Your life with Him - Your love for Him [2]
And freedom

Freedom to love - free to be loved

1. Psalm 118:5, Galatians 5:1

2. Galatians 5:13

Forgiveness - The essence of love

The essence of love, is waking up every morning and
experiencing the sun rising and realizing
that you had absolutely nothing to do with it

It's just there for you - you can't stop it, change it or
Ever make it better, regardless of what religion you are [1]

When night comes and you go to sleep again
No matter what you did that day or who you did it to
the sun will rise again- for them and for you
That's love - that's forgiveness - The essence of love

As God has forgiven you - forgive others [2]
Be a new morning for another person
Treat them like they are a new morning for you [3]
Be a participant in the love of every new morning from God.

That's love - that's God -   The essence of love [4]

1. Job 38-39, 40:1-4   2. Matthew 6:12-14

3. Galatians 6:1,2,   4. Luke 23:34

Be a Godly lover

Love encompasses itself and cannot be permeated or altered. Godly Love itself, has the power to permeate and to alter both the giver and the receiver.

When you know Godly love and you love in a Godly way, it will be evident to others, when you've chosen another over yourself.

True love, truly belongs to God. Love Him for what He represents - love, truth, forgiveness, unity and reconciliation and represent Him with those traits.

Being a Godly Lover requires actions of the spirit of God.

Active Spirit and truth - Godly lovers truly possess both.

Eternal love

It is pointless - aimless - fruitless - heartless

To look for a greater love [1]

There is nothing above God's goodness

Or greater than His loving kindness [2]

His love is timeless and tame less

Faultless and endless

You can't change eternal love

You just love it.

1. John 15:13

2. Exodus 15:13

May the Lord be with you

May the peace of the Lord

That passes all understanding

Guide and be with you [1]

May the word of the Lord

His love and commanding

Be in the words that you say

May His presence be on you [2]

And His light go before you

To brighten the path of your way

1. Philippians 4:7. 2. Numbers 6:25

125

A new beginning

Finally brethren, farewell. Be perfect, be of good comfort, be of one mind, live in peace; and the God of love and peace shall be with you.
2 Corinthians 13:11

The beginning started the journey - the end will be the beginning of another journey.
God's love never ends.

Sleep in Peace - Awake in love

Mark C. Ettinger

Scriptures of Love

KJV (paraphrased)

Love Scriptures

Leviticus 19:18 You shall not avenge, nor bear any grudge against the children of your people, but you shall love your neighbor as yourself: I am the LORD.

Leviticus 19:34 But the stranger that dwells with you shall be unto you as one born among you, and you shall love him as yourself.

Deuteronomy 6:5 And you shall love the LORD God with all your heart, and with all your soul, and with all your might. for you were strangers in the land of Egypt: I am the LORD your God.

Psalms 116:1 I love the LORD, because he heard my voice and my supplications.

Psalms 119:97 O how love I your law! it is my meditation all the day.

Proverbs 8:17 I love them that love me; and those that seek me early shall find me.

Proverbs 10:12 Hatred stirs up strife: but love covers all sins.

Song of Solomon 1:2 Let him kiss me with the kisses of his mouth: for his love is better than wine.
Song of Solomon 2:4 He brought me to the banqueting house, and his banner over me was love.

Song of Solomon 8:7 Many waters cannot quench love, neither can the floods drown it: if a man would give all the substance of his house for love, it would utterly be condemned.

Isaiah 56:6 Also the sons of the stranger, that join themselves to the LORD, to serve him, and to love the name of the LORD, to be his servants, every one that keeps the Sabbath from polluting it, and takes hold of my covenant;

Isaiah 66:10 Rejoice with Jerusalem, and be glad with her, all that love her: rejoice for joy with her, all that mourn for her:

Jeremiah 31:3 The LORD hath appeared of old unto me, saying, Yes, I have loved you with an everlasting love: therefore with loving kindness have I drawn you.

Ezekiel 33:31 And they come unto you as the people come, and they sit before you as my people, and they hear your words, but they will not do them: for with their mouth they show much love, but their heart goes after their covetousness.

Micah 6:8 He hath shown you, O man, what is good; and what doth the LORD require of you, but to do justly, and to love mercy, and to walk humbly with your God?

Zephaniah 3:17 The LORD thy God in the midst of you is mighty; he will save, he will rejoice over you with joy; he will rest in his love, he will joy over you with singing.

Matthew 5:44 But I say unto you, Love your enemies, bless them that curse you, do good to them that hate you, and pray for them which despitefully use you, and persecute you.

Matthew 5:46 For if you love them which love you, what reward do you have ? Do not even the publicans the same?

Matthew 19:19 Honor thy father and thy mother: and, You shall love your neighbor as yourself.

John 10:17 Therefore my Father loves me, because I lay down my life, that I might take it up again.

John 13:34 A new commandment I give unto you, That you love one another; as I have loved you, that you also love one another.

John 15:13 Greater love hath no man than this, that a man lay down his life for his friends.

John 17:26 And I have declared unto them your name, and will declare it: that the love which you have loved me may be in them, and I in them.

Romans 5:8 But God commends his love toward us, in that, while we were yet sinners, Christ died for us.

Romans 8:28 And we know that all things work together for good to them that love God, to them who are the called according to his purpose.

Romans 8:35   Who shall separate us from the love of Christ? shall tribulation, or distress, or persecution, or famine, or nakedness, or peril, or sword?

Romans 8:39   Nor height, nor depth, nor any other creature, shall be able to separate us from the love of God, which is in Christ Jesus our Lord.

Romans 12:9   Let love be without dissimulation. Abhor that which is evil; cleave to that which is good.

Romans 13:10   Love works no ill to his neighbor: therefore love is the fulfilling of the law.

1 Corinthians 2:9   But as it is written, Eye has not seen, nor ear heard, neither have entered into the heart of man, the things which God has prepared for them that love him.

1 Corinthians 4:21   What will you have? shall I come unto you with a rod, or in love, and in the spirit of meekness?

1 Corinthians 13:13   And now abide faith, hope, charity, these three; but the greatest of these is love,

2 Corinthians 13:11   Finally, brethren, farewell. Be perfect, be of good comfort, be of one mind, live in peace; and the God of love and peace shall be with you.

Galatians 5:22   But the fruit of the Spirit is love, joy, peace, longsuffering, gentleness, goodness, faith,

Ephesians 2:4   But God, who is rich in mercy, for it is with his great love that he loved us.

Ephesians 3:17 That Christ may dwell in your hearts by faith; that you, being rooted and grounded in love,

Ephesians 3:19 And to know the love of Christ, which passes knowledge, that you might be filled with all the fullness of God.

Ephesians 5:2 And walk in love, as Christ also hath loved us, and has given himself for us an offering and a sacrifice to God for a fragrance.

Ephesians 5:25 Husbands, love your wives, even as Christ also loved the church, and gave himself for it;

Ephesians 5:28 So ought men to love their wives as their own bodies. He that loves his wife loves himself.

Ephesians 5:33 Nevertheless let every one of you in particular so love his wife even as himself; and the wife see that she reverence her husband.

1 Timothy 6:10 For the love of money is the root of all evil: which while some coveted after, they have erred from the faith, and pierced themselves through with many sorrows. if any bowels and mercies,

1 Timothy 6:10 For the love of money is the root of all evil: which while some coveted after, they have erred from the faith, and pierced themselves through with many sorrows.

2 Timothy 1:7 For God hath not given us the spirit of fear; but of power, and of love, and of a sound mind.